UPSIDE DOWN LIVING

sabbath

[
The Upside-Down Living series emphasizes living out
one's Christian faith through the lens of Jesus
by following values that seem so countercultural
they appear to be upside down.
]

Anita Amstutz

Herald Press
Harrisonburg, Virginia

Upside-Down Living
Sabbath

Written by Anita Amstutz
Design by Merrill Miller
Cover photo by Laur-Kalevi Tamm/iStockphoto/Thinkstock/
   composite image

For orders or information, call 1-800-245-7894 or visit
HeraldPress.com.

20 19 18 17 16   10 9 8 7 6 5 4 3 2 1

[Contents]

[Introduction]

People in our churches struggle to connect with the holy on Sunday. Like our schools, our homes, and our public gathering places, we often become spectators in a sea of noise, words, busyness, and media. Yet we remain hungry for true connection. There is a soul sickness in our wealth-centered economy, partisan politics, and polarized culture. We continue to wonder at the roots of our depression, loneliness, and anxiety as a society.

The heart and soul of the Sabbath is to reconnect us—to ourselves, to one another, to our Maker. Sabbath is not only about ceasing work; it is about the redemption of our relationships, our work, our society, our economic system, our lifestyles, and time itself.

Shabbat, the Hebrew word for Sabbath, originated in Genesis. According to the divine example in Genesis 2, it was a day of ceasing one's labor in order to rest and celebrate the goodness of creation. After the people fled slavery in Egypt for the wilderness, Sabbath became a command. It took 40 years of exile for Yahweh to again become the center of their universe. Trust and obedience didn't come easy. Eventually, Sabbath became part of the Mosaic Law, and over the centuries a whole body of how-to lists sprang up around it.

Jesus, in the lineage of the prophets, stripped down all the added baggage, and reclaimed Sabbath from what had become a burdensome yoke on the people. Ultimately, the day was for healing, wholeness, and life. Humans were not created for Sabbath, but rather Sabbath for humans.

Today, Sabbath has been largely lost to us as 21st-century Christians. Unplugging from our technological, work-centered lives is difficult. It feels foreign to stop. Whether or not we attend worship, Sunday is seen as a day to do as we please.

So come and dwell in the heart of Sabbath awhile. Learn of what troubles your soul, and learn what makes your heart sing. This study is a call to return to the practice of Sabbath keeping, following values that seem so countercultural that they appear to be upside down. Let it replenish and restore, recreate us anew as the people of God.

—Anita Amstutz

1: SABBATH AS
Ceasing Work

[Genesis 1–2:2]

The Hebrew word Shabbat represents one of the
least understood and most important days instituted by
God. Literally meaning "to cease, to end, to rest,"[1] it swaps
out six task-oriented, building, and creating days for a
time of rest and spiritual enrichment on the seventh day.
The Ten Commandments call for not only *remembering*
(Exodus 20:8), but *observing* Sabbath (Deuteronomy 5:12).

1   "Shabbat," Judaism 101, accessed November 8, 2016,
http://www.jewfaq.org/shabbat.htm.

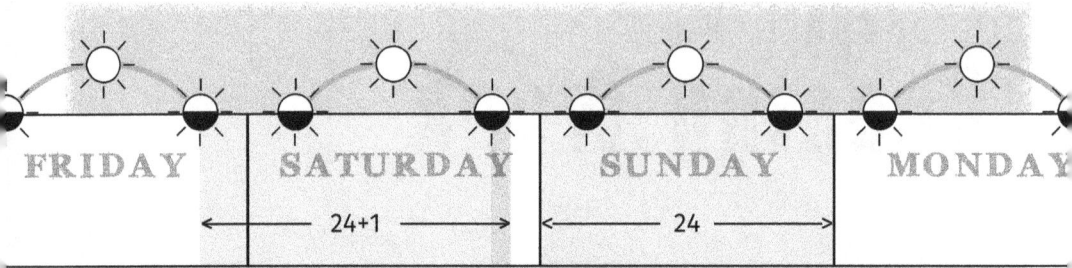

FRIDAY · SATURDAY · SUNDAY · MONDAY

← 24+1 → ← 24 →

Jewish Shabbat begins at sundown on Friday and lasts 25 hours.
It begins on Sunday morning for Christians, and lasts 24 hours.
It is a day to completely cease labor.

Sabbath first shows up in Genesis 2:2 as an exemplary way to end a work project! The author features Yahweh resting as a great way to kick back and reflect after seven days of a gigantic earth-making project.

The Sabbath imperative is not to accomplish or initiate anything, refuting the belief that you have to do something to be worthy. Instead, Sabbath calls us to cease doing something, acquiring things, expecting returns, so we can just *be* and receive the Creator's good gifts.

FORGET STIFLING RESTRICTIONS;
Sabbath is a precious gift from God.
Time for your body to stretch and your heart to sing.

In her book *Mudhouse Sabbath*, Lauren Winner cites a story of an Orthodox Hasidic family.

> In Liz Harris's *Holy Days*, a journalistic ethnography of a Hasidic family in Crown Heights, New York, Harris, a secular Jew, has come . . . to spend Shabbat with the Konigsbergs. She is perplexed, and a little annoyed, by all the restrictions. Over dinner, she asks her hosts why God cares whether or not she microwaves a frozen dinner on Friday night.
>
> "What happens when we stop working and controlling nature?" Moishe Konigsberg responds. "When we don't operate machines, or pick flowers, or pluck fish from the sea? . . . When we cease interfering in the world, we are acknowledging that it is God's world."[2]

In other words, we are invited to give up our illusion of control and to appreciate that God is in charge. Sabbath is "an alternative to the demanding, chattering, pervasive presence of advertising and the . . . liturgical claim of professional sports that devour all our rest time . . . [it is] the most difficult and urgent commandment in our society because it summons us to intent and conduct that defies our commodity-propelled society that specializes in control, entertainment, bread, and circuses . . . along with anxiety and violence."[3]

Sabbath, then, becomes a reorienting of priorities about whose world it is and with whom we cocreate. Without this understanding we get sick in body and soul—a spiritual sickness that is infecting our whole society.

---

2   Winner, *Mudhouse Sabbath* (Brewster, MA: Paraclete Press, 2003), 6–7.
3   Walter Brueggemann, *Sabbath as Resistance: Saying No to the Culture of Now* (Louisville, KY: Westminster John Knox Press, 2014), xiv.

Sabbath is characterized by **kairos** time. Mary, the mother of Jesus, received the angel Gabriel's announcement that she was to carry the Son of God. This was just such a *kairos* moment—a Greek word meaning the opportune time or the right season. Mary's annunciation was ripe with transformation, and fraught with crisis. **It was God-time, pregnant with potential**.

> [SABBATH CALLS US to return
>   week after week and remember.]

Ceasing work allows us to slow down and see opportune, present moments with new eyes. It is that flower before you, your child's breath, the paint on the canvas, the song you are singing. It is eternal time, different from our usual busy, measured wrist-watch time that traps us into believing we are truly living.

But like Mary, it can also bring us to an exciting and terrifying brink in our lives—face-to-face with a new understanding. Empty time might open up new frontiers of restlessness and show us the disturbance driving our soul to stay busy. Perhaps that is why we are not so eager to cease our labor.

Fallow time allows us to let our hair down, so to speak, and just *be*. For children, idle time is necessary to stimulate imagination and provide space to create. For adults, it seems that some of the best inventions have come from daydreaming and space to reflect—opening up vast reservoirs of creativity and joy.

We tend to glorify our work stations (I'm a banker, writer, lawyer, doctor, pastor, biologist, teacher, nurse). We teach our children to make work and money central to our lives.

What if it became a regular time to celebrate our everyday lives as connected to God's time—our self-worth beyond a mere category? When work is braided in and out of the sacred weekly rhythms of Sabbath time—worship, idle time, the grace of sleep, prayer, play, eating together—perhaps our being will move in sync with the Lord of life rather than our titles or reputation. As we participate in the larger God pattern of Sabbath, our work will cease to consume our lives. And as work is shrunk down to size, God has a chance to become our center of gravity.

> **What if Sabbath became central?**

In conclusion, the aim of God's work in the world is not about the almighty dollar or bottom line. Rather, it is about the rhythm of good work that ends every seven days, in order to revel in and enjoy life's sweetness. This rhythm of ceasing work weekly can reprioritize our life. Holy rest gives us a chance to participate with God in reflecting on all that is good—no longer striving to *be good*. Ceasing our relentless striving allows a new upside-down reality to bubble up. For Jews, who knew enslavement to work, it is often said, "More than Israel has kept Shabbat, Shabbat has kept Israel."

[Talk about It]

▶ Share your experiences of Sabbath from childhood. How has it formed and shaped your habits of Sabbath keeping today?

▶ Take a few minutes to journal about the subject of "My Brief History of Work." What does work mean to you? Has Sabbath shaped and formed your work life? If so, how? If not, how might it change your work habits and thoughts about work in your life now?

▶ Have you ever experienced that *kairos* time when you consciously unplugged from clock time? What was this like?

▶ What if Sabbath became central to the life of you and your family? How might it allow you to reorient and reprioritize your life?

2: SABBATH AS
[Coming Home]

[Deuteronomy 6:1-9]

Are you a stranger to your soul comings and goings these days? Does a sense of meaninglessness, depression, or irritation lurk around the edges?

Our lives are out of balance and we have lost connection with our very souls. No one knows this better than the millennial generation. They see a future mortgaged by debt and militarism, institutions no longer relevant, and a planet devastated by generations who have overdrawn the natural resources account. And so they refuse the broken, industrialized systems that are no longer sustainable. "Work less, live more" is their cry as they build tiny houses, evade the debt-peddling salespeople, and live lower on the food chain.

> Coming home to our souls is at the root of Deuteronomy 6:4-9, and the verses are known as the *Shema*.[1] Stop running after everything around you. Slow down. Dwell awhile. Love the Lord your God with all your heart, soul, and strength. Tell your children. Write it on your forehead and doorframes and tie it on your wrists.

There is a story of a child who was found by his panicked mother, who thought him lost in a busy train station: "There he was, hunkered down in rapt attention listening to a scruffy old man play a lonely mouth organ in the cold rain." When the mother found her son, he was offering his last coins "to his new hero, oblivious to the man's appearance. 'How lucky he is,' he said to his [mom], his eyes shining, 'to be able to play such beautiful music.' [This child] was listening with the ear of his heart."[2]

Jesus often referred to children as showing us the way to where the kingdom lay, close at hand. Children, who have not yet been over-socialized. Children, who are still fresh from God. Children, whose souls are still enlivened by the divine presence all around us. Children, who call us home to our souls.

Morton Kelsey writes, "An efficiently busy life, which keeps us occupied without being harried and keeps our attention entirely on interesting outer things, is probably more potentially destructive of spiritual growth than debauchery or alcohol or hard drugs. . . . On the other hand, a quiet, efficient and busy life spent

---

1   The Shema, Deuteronomy 6:4-9, is one of only two prayers that are specifically commanded in Torah (the other is Birkat Ha-Mazon—grace after meals). It is the oldest fixed daily prayer in Judaism, recited morning and night since ancient times.
2   Daniel O'Leary, "Threshold of the Soul," *Tablet*, April 24, 2010, 7, http://archive.thetablet.co.uk/article/24th-april-2010/7/threshold-of-the-soul.

continuously in good works can shield an individual most effectively from any plunge into the depths where God dwells."[3]

To love God with all our heart, soul, and strength is

ultimately to know ourselves as beloved. The gift of this belovedness lies in the stopping of our own clever schemes and schedules to rest with the fullness of God for a time. It is a plenitude of enough. The temple of your body and soul cannot be whole and complete inside the acquiring mind of culture and our economy.

For the first-century Jewish community, Sabbath often fell prey to picky purity rules by religious leaders, rather than remaining an invitation to dwell in God's love for 25 hours. Paul's communities during the time of the Roman Empire struggled to define themselves by the kingdom within rather than the political world around. In his letters from prison to the far-flung church at Colossae, he described Jesus Christ as the Lord of all (Colossians 1:15-20).

> One must step outside for a while and inhabit Sabbath time, carving out God space in our beleaguered lives and the bewildering politics of our times. It is our touchstone to reconnect with the Lord of all, a place of peace.

As 21st-century people, we are also dulled

and entranced by the world we live within. When we cease our human-generated activity, we enter a "palace in time," as Rabbi Abraham Heschel calls it.[4] Here is a place saturated with the divine presence, ready to redeem and recreate our lives and our busy schedules. The Lord of all is awaiting our return, ready to set our feet in a new direction.

We need to take time to retreat from our busy lives so that we can meet God. If we only work, then we begin to think that work is all that matters, and that we live to keep our work going.

---

3   Kelsey, *The Other Side of Silence* (New York: Paulist Press, 1976), 83.
4   Heschel, *The Sabbath* (New York: Farrar, Straus & Giroux, 1951).

[We need to take time to remember
the relationship we have with God,
who dwells within our soul.]

In conclusion, home is where the soul can be at peace. Sabbath keeping can call us back to dwell for a while in our soul's home. This is a place in time where we can reconnect with the living God, who has ordered all things and still calls us beloved.

[Talk about It]

▶ Journal about the ways in which your busy life may be keeping you from remembering that God dwells in your soul.

▶ Share an experience when you were able to dwell with the Lord of Sabbath and feel a homecoming to your soul.

▶ Have you ever experienced Sabbath as a legalistic set of rules? What might you do to redeem that experience and reclaim Sabbath keeping as life giving?

3: SABBATH AS
God's Economy

[Exodus 16:1-32; Leviticus 25; Micah 6:8]

Sabbath is not purely spiritual. It is a cultural resistance to insatiable production. God's economy is about enough. It is about celebrating abundance, sharing, rest, and trust. To surrender a whole day to God can begin to transform desires and longings rooted in an unjust, acquisition-oriented economic system. It is disengaging from an empire voraciously eating up human and physical resources 24/7.

> **Sabbath cries "Time out!" to examine these things in our life:**
> - The slavery of credit
> - A growing chasm between rich and poor
> - Rapacious destruction of our planet
> - An economic and military machine
> - Technology and media consumption

Like the Hebrews in Egypt, we are exiles in a strange land. They were called into the wilderness to remember who, and whose, they were. First on the agenda was Sabbath Economics 101, complete with manna and quails. They were relearning to trust God, not mammon. Likewise, Sabbath prepares us to remember whom, and what, we have neglected. To reenter our worlds again "to do justice, and to love kindness, and to walk humbly with your God" (Micah 6:8).

Tim Kreider, the author of *We Learn Nothing*, in an essay entitled "The Busy Trap," writes, "If you live in America in the 21st century you've probably had to listen to a lot of people tell you how busy they are. It's become the default response when you ask anyone how they're doing: 'Busy!' '*So* busy.' '*Crazy* busy!' It's pretty obviously a boast disguised as a complaint."[1]

Kreider believes it's a class thing. Working-class folks pulling back-to-back shifts or commuting by bus to three minimum wage jobs are not busy. They are tired. Exhausted. Dead on their feet. They don't see a Sabbath on the horizon anytime soon.

---

1   *New York Times Sunday Review*, July 1, 2012,
http://opinionator.blogs.nytimes.com/2012/06/30/the-busy-trap/?_r=0.

Busy, busy, busy: Where does our time go?

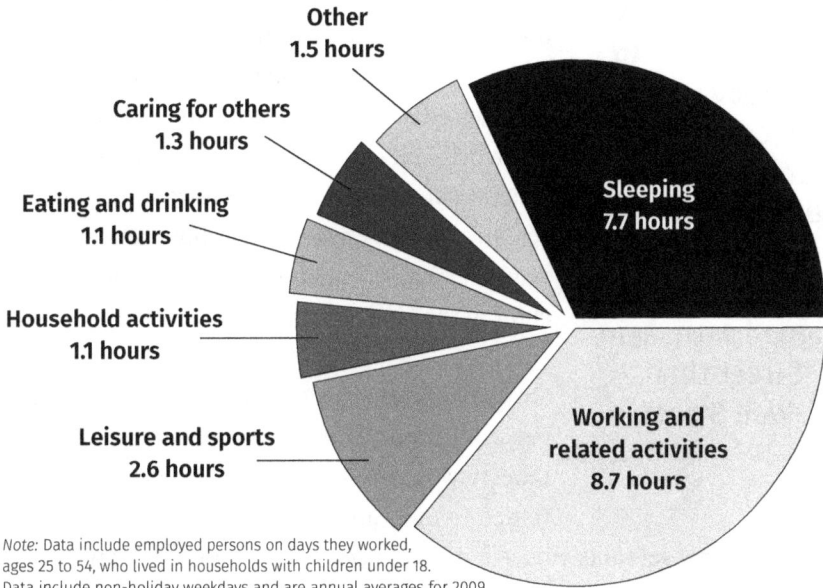

Other
1.5 hours

Caring for others
1.3 hours

Eating and drinking
1.1 hours

Household activities
1.1 hours

Leisure and sports
2.6 hours

Sleeping
7.7 hours

Working and
related activities
8.7 hours

Note: Data include employed persons on days they worked,
ages 25 to 54, who lived in households with children under 18.
Data include non-holiday weekdays and are annual averages for 2009.
Source: Bureau of Labor Statistics

Over the centuries, many peoples have been marginalized
and disenfranchised by Western Christendom's ambitious rush to
conquer, divide, and control. In 1452, the Doctrine of Discovery
charged all explorers of "new lands" to "invade, capture, vanquish
and subdue . . . all Saracens (Muslims), Pagans and all enemies of
Christ . . . to reduce their persons to perpetual slavery . . . and to
take away all their possessions and property."[2] This legalized theft
of land, labor, and resources continues. Indigenous peoples across
the world are systematically denied their human rights. These 15th-
century laws are underpinnings of our Western economic and le-
gal system today, still cited to justify extraction and land grabs.

Our economic machine is still hard at work oppressing many.

---

2   Sarah Augustine and Katerina Friesen, "Dismantling the Doctrine of
Discovery" (fact sheet), Dismantling the Doctrine of Discovery, accessed
November 8, 2016, https://doctrineofdiscoverymenno.files.wordpress
.com/2015/06/dod_factsheet1.pdf.

[As Christians, we are called to embody God's economy, a paradigm distinctly different from the dominant paradigm, more aligned with Main Street than Wall Street.]

The ancient Sabbath economics master plan in Leviticus 25 critiqued an economic system that dispossessed the vulnerable—allowing property and possession to be bought, sold, traded, used, and abused at their expense. This Sabbath plan was a brilliant cast of sevens to create balance, perspective, and equity. The Hebrews would not only cease work every seventh day, but every seven years there also would be a grand rest for all, including the land, servants, and animals.

On the 50th year (seven times seven), the trumpet would sound on the Day of Atonement. Liberty would be proclaimed. Everyone would return to their ancestral land, including slaves and servants whose land had been seized for debt repayment. The vulnerable who were dispossessed would be compensated. It was Sabbath economics, God style.

To understand the roots of God's Sabbath economics we must return to the story of the enslaved Israelites, who made bricks for Pharaoh's empire and its hungry beast of production.[3] It took Moses and the burning bush to lead them into 40 years

DAYS	YEARS	7 YEARS
1	1	1–7
2	2	8–14
3	3	15–21
4	4	22–28
5	5	29–35
6	6	36–42
Shabbat	Shabbat	43–49
		50: Jubilee

---

3   Exodus 1 and 5 chronicle the oppression of the Hebrews by Pharaoh.

of wilderness exile where they reacquainted themselves with the Lord of Shabbat. Even so, it was not easy to crack the internal oppression that the god of imperial wealth had imprinted. God's Sabbath economy in Exodus 16 included manna and quails, valuing people, trust, and covenant more than endless production.[4] "This God is subsequently revealed as a God of mercy, steadfast love, and faithfulness who is committed to covenantal relationships of fidelity. . . . At the taproot of this divine commitment to relationship (covenant) rather than commodity (bricks) is the capacity and willingness of this God to rest."[5]

In Exodus 20:8, the Sabbath became codified into the Mosaic Law. Eventually the grand design for Sabbath fell into disrepair as Israel alternated between captivity in Babylon and its very own empire.

> [**Sabbath is not a tame Sunday morning requirement.**]

In conclusion, to practice Sabbath is a subversive act of biblical justice. It begins to loosen the gods of production and acquisition that have a stranglehold on all of us. It is a healthy alternative to a culture gone amok, grasping for more, more, more. It is a relief for those who are weary and burdened by incessant activity and debt—a rebalancing. A return to God's Sabbath economics will threaten to liberate us from the steroid demands of the "fleshpots of Egypt" (Exodus 16:3). It will retrain our habits, decolonize our minds, and unbind the chains of our hearts. In God's world we are not the dominators.

---

4 Exodus 6:1-8 is a reminder of God's covenant and promise of deliverance.
5 Brueggemann, *Sabbath as Resistance*, 6.

> The bottom line of God's Sabbath economy is ultimately relationship and covenant— not profit—calling us to justice and mercy.

[Talk about It]

▶ What might be some of the "fleshpots of Egypt" (Exodus 16:3) that we pin our security upon in society today? In your life?

▶ God's manna-and-quail Sabbath economy was revealed to the Israelites as they were led into the wilderness. Share a wilderness story from your own life or church experience that illustrates a deepening season of trust and obedience in God.

▶ How might your church incorporate the Sabbath master design of sevens (seven days, seven years, and Jubilee) to live out the Micah mandate to "to do justice, and to love kindness, and to walk humbly with your God" (Micah 6:8)?

▶ Moses asked Aaron to preserve an omer of manna in a jar so that generations to come could see that the Lord was faithful. Share how your church might preserve and pass along God's Sabbath economy of relationship and covenant to future generations.

4: SABBATH AS
Healing

[Mark 2:23-3:5; Luke 13:10-17]

Through the ages, Sabbath has fallen prey to a sinkhole of legalisms. Some Christians remember the Lord's Day as "thou shalt nots" and gratefully washed their hands of Sabbath, leaving it behind as adults.

[Jesus' work was about reinitiating religious rules and regulations that had lost their deeper meaning. Sabbath was one of them.]

The Jewish people ceased their labor, but over time they picked up another list of shoulds and should nots. These included instructions on burnt offerings, how much water could be poured, what to wear, caring for animals, and restriction of movement on travel, harvesting, and kindling of fires.[1]

> [To end this oppression, Jesus made it clear that humans weren't created for the Sabbath, but Sabbath was created for humans.]

For Jesus, observing Sabbath did not preclude caring for those who suffered. Keeping the Sabbath was actually a celebration and a life-affirming act—God's intention for this day set apart.

As churchgoers, we don't fear that our religious leaders or God will strike us down if we don't keep a 24-hour Sabbath. **But perhaps the more important question is,** have we lost the heart of the Sabbath, which can actually bring a healing balm to our work-weary souls? What if Sabbath were actually about "I get to . . . !"?

Barbara Brown Taylor, an Episcopal minister, began keeping Sabbath regularly. After seven years, she could attest to the struggle to rest the first few years. Her mind paced with questions about what was kosher on Sabbath. Could she dig in her garden? Throw in some laundry? After a few years, she noticed that she depended on Sabbath as an integral part of her life; as necessary as eating and breathing. She worked hard six days, knowing that that the seventh was on its way.

---

1 *Jewish Encyclopedia*, s.v. "Sabbath," by Emil G. Hirsh et al., accessed November 8, 2016, http://jewishencyclopedia.com/articles/12962-sabbath.

With sundown on the Sabbath I stopped seeing the dust
balls, the bills and the laundry. They were still there but they
had lost their power over me. One day each week I lived as
if all my work were done. I loved as if the kingdom had come
and when I did the kingdom came, for 25 hours at least.
Now when I know Sabbath is near, I can feel the anticipation
bubbling up inside of me. Sabbath is no longer a good idea
or even a spiritual discipline . . . it is an experience of divine
love that swamps both body and soul."[2]

Three of the synoptic gospels tell the story of the man
with the withered hand, the one whom Jesus healed on the
Sabbath.

Prior to this Sabbath healing in Mark 3, Jesus'
ire had been kindled time and again by the
Pharisaical attitudes of a rigid Sabbath law. He
had just had a run-in with the religious bean
counters who judged him for plucking grain with
his disciples to eat as they walked. Jesus reminded
them that even the celebrated warrior king David
shared the very food off the altar with his com-
panions on the Sabbath. Food is life. Life is more
important than laws.

> The healing
> work of
> Sabbath begins
> as we reimagine
> and practice it as
> a source of joy,
> celebration,
> and healing—
> not drudgery.

The man with the withered hand was set free
in body and spirit on the Sabbath. Now this day would have
new meaning as a place and time where Jesus made him whole.
Sabbath was indeed a day to participate in life to the fullest and in
a vocation of praising God!

We are also a people needing to be made whole in our minds,
bodies, and spirits. **Healing is not a one-time deal**. Week by

2   Taylor, "Sabbath Resistance," in *Christian Century*, May 31, 2005, 35.

week, life hands us struggles, sorrows, and burdens. Sabbath is the place where Jesus meets us again and again as we keep coming back to be restored to our right mind and body. It is no coincidence that Jesus healed on the Sabbath—not only in this story, but also in the story of the woman crippled for 18 long years (Luke 13:10-17). Healing paired with Sabbath sends an important message of what is essential for this day—both then and now.

The Greek word used in the Mark 3 healing story and continually throughout the Gospels is **SÓZÓ**. As the root of Savior and salvation, *sózó* literally means to save, heal, preserve, and rescue.[3]

In Mark's story of the man with the shriveled hand, when faced with the accusations of healing on the Sabbath, Jesus asked, "What is lawful on the Sabbath: to do good or to do evil, to save life or kill?" Without an answer, he proceeded to restore the man to wholeness. Jesus knew the heavy yokes his people carried, not only with the Roman occupation but also with the religious laws of the day. He came to free the oppressed.

In conclusion, Jesus remembered the true heart of the Sabbath for all time. Healing of one's body, mind, and soul brought glory to God and was central to observing this day—not legalistic rules. We are invited to fully inhabit Sabbath so that healing can take place as we return week after week.

> [A Jesus-style Sabbath can heal and restore us to all that is life affirming. It is a celebration of wholeness and salvation!]

3   *Strong's Concordance*, s.v. "sózó," accessed November 8, 2016, http://www.biblehub.com/greek/4982.htm.

[Talk about It]

▶ Do you have any memories in your family or church story of Sabbath legalisms? Take a moment to journal about how these stories affected you. If Sabbath legalisms were not passed along to you, journal about your own teaching, understanding, and experience of Sabbath.

▶ What comes up for you when you consider keeping Sabbath for a complete 25 hours on a regular basis, as Barbara Brown Taylor has done? Can you imagine doing this for years?

▶ One of the meanings of the Greek word *sózó* is "to heal." As this word shows up over and over in the New Testament, how does this reframe your understanding of salvation and Jesus' saving work of reclaiming the Sabbath for healing throughout the Gospels?

▶ Do you identify with any of the persons Jesus encountered in the Sabbath healing stories—Pharisees concerned for piety, eating what you shouldn't on the Sabbath, a man with a withered hand, a woman with a spirit that had crippled her for 18 years? How have you experienced Jesus' healing touch or freedom from oppression?

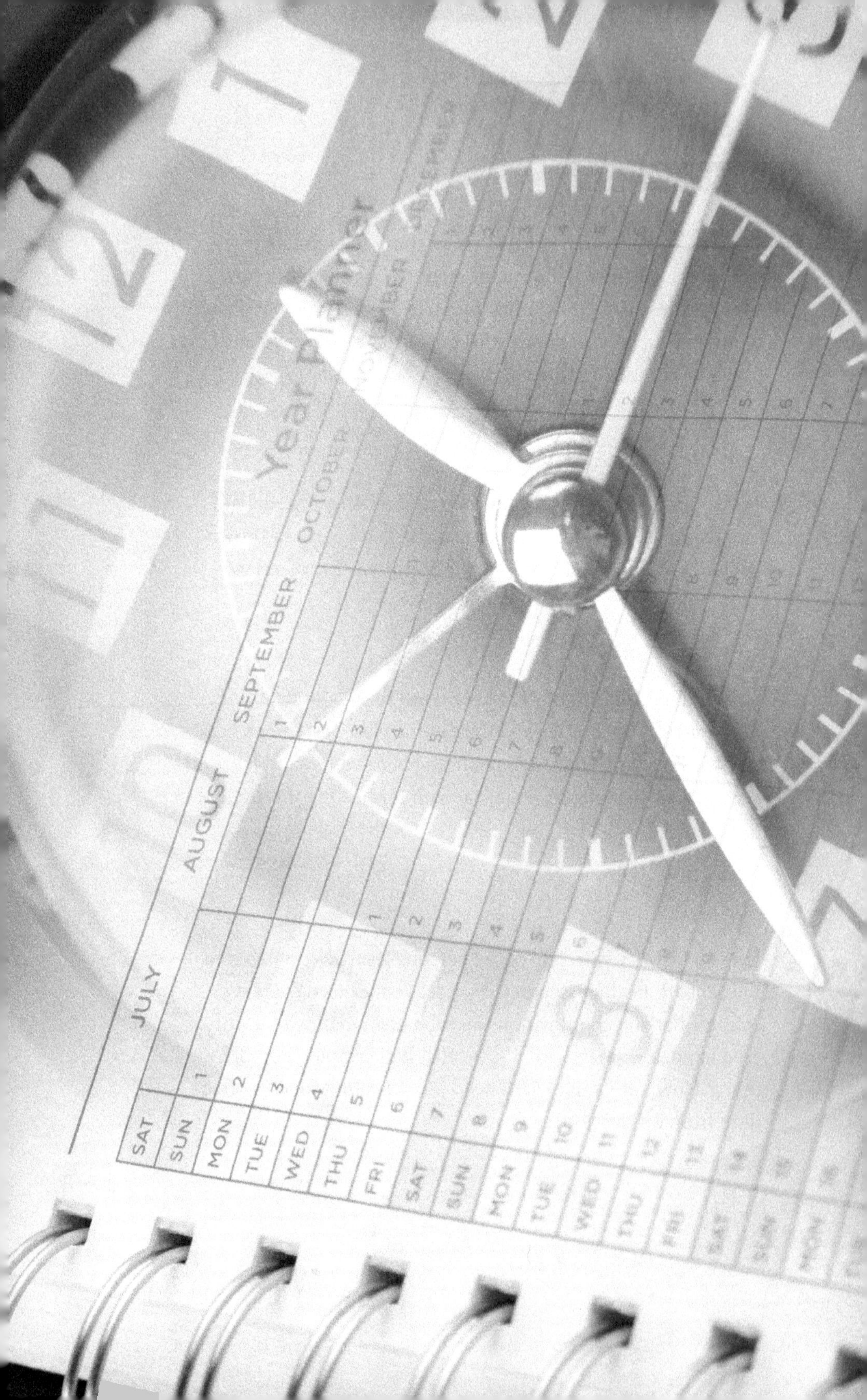
JULY
AUGUST
SEPTEMBER
OCTOBER

5: SABBATH AS
[a Hospitality of Time]

[Luke 10:38-42]

What would happen if North American Christians
spent as many hours weekly doing church together as
they do sitting alone in front of a screen? A churchwide
renewal could break out if we took a Wednesday night
media Sabbath—to unplug and spend face-to-face time in
agape feasting, singing hymns, and dwelling in the Word.

In the story of Mary and Martha, Jesus invites Martha to re-
lease her burden of *doing* to spend cherished time with him.
Jesus modeled such time spent in table fellowship with all kinds
of people—a foretaste of the great feast of God's kingdom. In
times such as these, when massive shifts and stressors in our
society strain us and we struggle with conflict and polarization,
time spent in the art of conversation and shared food can build
bridges of friendship and goodwill. We not only gather our

> [Jesus calls us to a Sabbath where a hospitality
> of time sweetens our relationships.]

beloveds around the table, but also welcome the stranger. It is a taste of the now, and the not yet. Eternal time.

Nan Fink's memoir, *Stranger in the Midst*, is the story of her conversion to Judaism upon marrying her husband. She describes the preparations for Sabbath as a frenzied beehive of activity, the storm before the calm, when everything would be completely ready as sundown approached. She writes:

> When I joined Michael and his son for the lighting of the candles, the whole house seemed transformed. Papers and books were neatly piled, flowers stood in a vase on the table, and the golden light of the setting sun filled the room . . . Shabbat is like nothing else. Time as we know it does not exist for these twenty-four hours, and the worries of the week soon fall away. A feeling of joy appears. The smallest object, a leaf or a spoon, shimmers in a soft light, and the heart opens. Shabbat is a meditation of unbelievable beauty.[1]

Generations going forward have lost the body memory, the craft, and most of all the time for this most basic, practical, and exquisite of domestic arts—welcoming Sabbath time over a meal. Making space for beauty, worship, and conversation.

> [Sabbath is a peaceful resistance to these forces. As we create space for Sabbath time, swapping personal stories over good food, listening, and being present to those we love, we take back the public narrative, rebalancing and reshaping our lives in the way of Jesus.]

---

1   Quoted in Winner, *Mudhouse Sabbath*, 2.

We face a cultural onslaught of media groupthink, spin, and partisan politics. It eats up our airspace together. Perhaps it forms and shapes us more than the gospel of Jesus Christ.

The New Testament story of Mary and Martha is often seen as a finger wag at Martha. She is stuck in the hosting details and Mary is the exemplary model. But perhaps Jesus' gentle chide is less a critique of Martha and more a tending to her frazzled soul. As he lifts up the need to let go of the worries of the day and come, sit, keep company, Jesus offers a critique to a time-starved culture that has lost its ability to be present and listen to one another.

Like our 21st-century generation, first-century Palestine dwellers were also consumed by tasks and distractions. It seems that Martha was feeling the burden of proper hosting and abandonment by her sister. But Jesus, in effect, called for an upside-down way of thinking about hospitality. As he noted Martha's list of worries and anxious presence, Jesus looked beyond the perfectly clean house or choicest meal.

> **Such real presence and connection is at a premium in our day.**

What truly mattered, the real feast to which he called Martha, and indeed us, is that timeless and eternal moment of connection between human beings, sitting down together, and sharing from the heart. Jesus said, **"Few things are needed—or indeed only one"** (Luke 10:42 NIV). Perhaps that one thing was the focused clarity of *presence* with another.

We mostly communicate with screens or sound bites. We pay for people to listen to us. We unconsciously hunger for the ease and time needed for a good story and heartfelt, honest conversation.

Number of U.S. adult users per month

AM/FM radio	240 Million
Live+DVR/time-shifted TV	226M
App/web on a smartphone	191M
Internet on a PC	162M
Time-shifted TV (DVR)	158M
Tablet	106M
DVD/Blu-ray	93M
Game console	61M
Multimedia device	60M

Source: Nielsen Total Audience Report, Q1 2016

In conclusion, a Sabbath hospitality of time is an oasis where we honor one another with our undivided presence. It is a place where the tasks and stressors are dropped for at least a complete day. The only requirement is showing up with our full self. Jesus asked no less of Martha.

[Talk about It]

▶ In the Martha and Mary story, who are you most like? Why?

▶ Talk about a meaningful "hospitality of time." When you have experienced this? When have you offered it? Was there a quality of presence and heartfelt connection that was different?

▶ Consider asking your family, friend, or spouse to observe a 24-hour Sabbath media fast with you. Engage them to come up with questions and topics for a heartfelt story or two when gathered around the table. How does this feel as you imagine doing this?

▶ Share your thoughts about whether a dedicated churchwide Sabbath keeping could revitalize your church community to follow in the way of Jesus.

6: SABBATH AS
Shalom

[Isaiah 65:17-25; Colossians 1:15-20; 2:16-17]

Shalom is well-being. It is peace. In a world wrecked by violence, war, and terrorism, shalom is a rare and precious state of being that hearkens back to the garden of Eden. Isaiah, the prophet of old, envisioned a new heaven and a new earth. The early Christians prayed for earth and heaven to be one. Anabaptists practiced pacifism as a sign of God's kingdom. Jewish brothers and sisters greet one another with "Shabbat shalom" as the candles are lit on Friday evening.

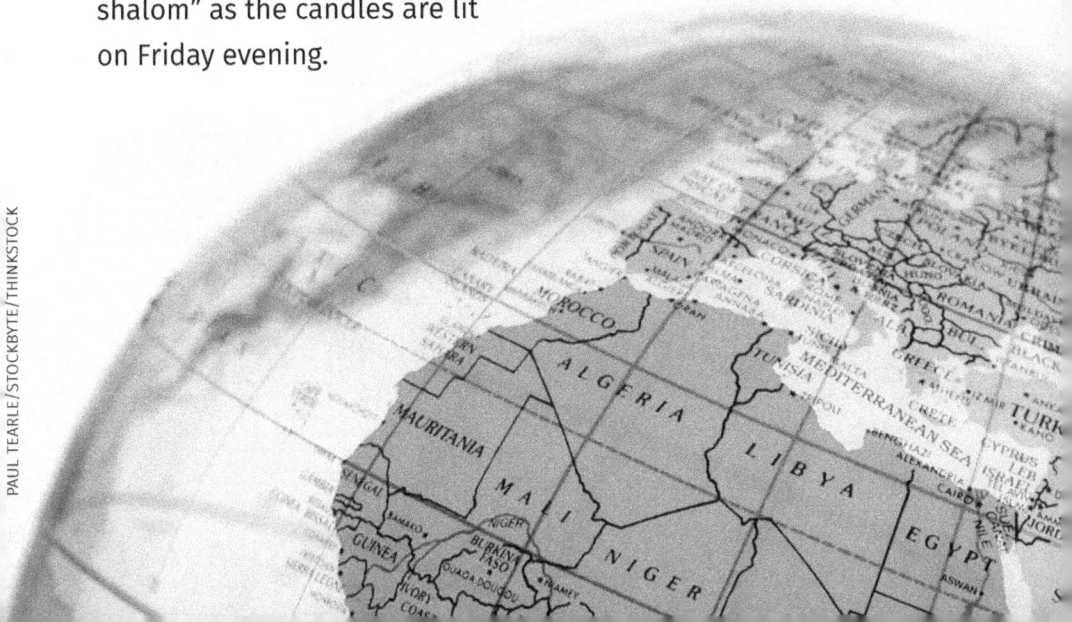

[Sabbath and shalom go hand in hand.]

For Christians, Sunday morning Sabbath is a time to renew minds and spirits within a worshiping community. But if it is only a rote activity with no deeper change of heart, it becomes a ritual, festival, or ceremonial law that God hates (Isaiah 1:13). "At its heart, Christian faith points toward a transformed understanding of reality itself. In Christian language, repentance (Greek **metanoia**) or conversion implies a fundamental 'turning around' . . . a fundamental change in our worldview."[1]

Yet, a fundamental change to our lifestyle is also required. If Sabbath keeping doesn't change us to become people of God's peace, it is a sham. Barbara Brown Taylor writes:

> In his book *Jewish Renewal*, Rabbi Michael Lerner says that anyone engaging in the practice of Shabbat can expect a rough ride for a couple of years at least. This is because Sabbath involves pleasure, rest, freedom, slowness, none of which comes naturally to North Americans. Most of us are so sold on speed, so invested in productivity, so convinced that multitasking is the way of life that stopping for one whole day can feel at first like a kind of death. . . . Two hours on Friday afternoon is not enough. . . . We need ten times longer than that to calm down enough to draw a deep breath. . . . "You haven't had the experience," he says, "until you've tried doing it for the full 25 hours, and doing it for a year or two minimum."[2]

---

1 Roth, *Choosing against War: A Christian View* (Intercourse, PA: Good Books, 2002), 35.
2 Taylor, "Sabbath Resistance," 35.

> For Christians, who understand that the risen Christ *is* our shalom, bringing us freedom and life abundant, Sabbath becomes a joyful opportunity to regularly wed ourselves to the Lord of the Sabbath—the One who makes all things new.

Despite this head knowledge, sometimes the physical practice and heart experience can take time, as Rabbi Lerner notes. It will require a change of life habits, and a more careful understanding of what you do and why you do what you do.

Paul wrote a letter to the Colossians, a Gentile church, praising Jesus Christ as the firstborn of all creation, the invisible God made visible, in whom all things hold together. Paul noted that Christ reconciles all things to himself in peace. Shalom comes through him.

Later in this same letter, Paul pleaded with the people not to become too pious or hung up on religious customs. Evidently, Gentiles were being pressed to observe Jewish customs, laws, and special days in order to be right with God. Paul said, "Therefore do not let anyone judge you by what you eat or drink, or with regard to a religious festival, a New Moon celebration or a Sabbath day. These are a shadow of the things that were to come; the reality however, is found in Christ" (Colossians 2:16-17 NIV).

For Paul, faith trumped works, Spirit was

at the heart of law, and Christ was at the center of all religious celebrations and rituals. Sabbath was only a shadow of the real deal.

> At the heart of Sabbath is Christ. The One who is reconciling all things to himself and recreating us in his image as peacemakers.

> [**The celebration of the Sabbath is to transform us totally and fully into who we are, hidden in Christ.**]

If Sabbath doesn't make us Christ's people of shalom, of wholeness and well-being, then perhaps it needs a closer examination, a change of heart. Sister Joan Chittister writes:

> There is an ancient monastic story about a religious person who, wanting to be holy, asked their spiritual guide: "According as I am able, I keep my little rule; I do my little fast, my prayer, my meditation, my contemplative silence, and according as I am able I strive to cleanse my heart from evil thoughts. Now, holy one, what more should I do?" The elder rose up, stretched her hands all the way to heaven, and her fingers became like ten lamps of fire. And the holy one said, "If you want to be holy, why not be totally changed into fire?"[3]

In conclusion, we are called to be peace to the world around us, in the way of Jesus. The practice of Sabbath only foreshadows the new heaven and new earth yet to come. If the practice of Sabbath doesn't call us to become new creations in Christ, a people of peace, then it is only an empty ritual.

> [**We become more and more fully people of shalom as we take time to come and dwell in the heart of Christ regularly.**]

---

3   Joan Chittister OSB, "Gifts of Fire," in *Preaching on Peace*, eds. Ronald Sider and Darrel J. Brubaker (Philadelphia: Fortress Press, 1982), 58.

[Talk about It]

▶ How might observing Sabbath regularly actually create shalom for you and your family? Talk about the difficulty of doing this as a regular practice for 24 hours each week.

▶ Clearly, Sabbath, like any other religious observance, can become an idol rather than the true meaning at the core. Can you name another religious observance on Sunday Sabbath that has become stale or rote for you?

▶ Journal about what "dwelling in the heart of Christ" means to you, and the fruits of this in your life.

▶ Consider how Sabbath could begin to change your community and even the world if Christ's shalom was seen at the heart of it.

Anita Amstutz is an ordained minister in Mennonite Church USA. She has a master of divinity degree and a master's degree in theology and the arts. Prior to becoming a pastor, Anita was a social worker who worked with the Head Start program, the homeless, and low-income neighborhoods.

After seminary, Anita was a pastor in Albuquerque, New Mexico. Sabbath became an important practice in the midst of an active ministry and the ups and downs of life. For over eight years, she has experimented with keeping a day set aside to practice Sabbath. It has helped her reclaim a more contemplative, mindful lifestyle, and find a peaceful place to land after a busy week. Sabbath has not only sweetened life itself, but strengthened spiritual discernment in decisions.

As an avid reader, writer, singer, and journaler, Sabbath is a perfect excuse for Anita to spend hours losing herself in any of these practices, along with hours of shared teatime or food with those she loves.

Anita still lives in New Mexico and keeps house with her husband, two feisty but sweet cats, and a yard full of honeybees. Her favorite way to keep Sabbath is in God's creation. Anita and her husband are often found hiking, biking, skiing, and ambling along on such days.